TRAMPOLINING

PHYSICAL EDUCATION ACTIVITIES SERIES

Consulting Editor:
AILEENE LOCKHART
University of Southern California
Los Angeles, California

Evaluation Materials Editor:
JANE A. MOTT
Smith College
Northampton, Massachusetts

ARCHERY, Wayne C. McKinney
BADMINTON, Margaret Varner Bloss
BADMINTON, ADVANCED, Wynn Rogers
BASKETBALL FOR MEN, Glenn Wilkes
BASKETBALL FOR WOMEN, Frances Schaafsma
BIOPHYSICAL VALUES OF MUSCULAR ACTIVITY, E. C. Davis,
    Gene A. Logan, and Wayne C. McKinney
BOWLING, Joan Martin
CANOEING AND SAILING, Linda Vaughn and Richard Stratton
CIRCUIT TRAINING, Robert P. Sorani
CONDITIONING AND BASIC MOVEMENT CONCEPTS, Jane A. Mott
CONTEMPORARY SQUARE DANCE, Patricia A. Phillips
FENCING, Muriel Bower and Torao Mori
FIELD HOCKEY, Anne Delano
FIGURE SKATING, Marion Proctor
FOLK DANCE, Lois Ellfeldt
GOLF, Virginia L. Nance and E. C. Davis
GYMNASTICS FOR MEN, A. Bruce Frederick
GYMNASTICS FOR WOMEN, A. Bruce Frederick
HANDBALL, Michael Yessis
ICE HOCKEY, Don Hayes
JUDO, Daeshik Kim
KARATE AND PERSONAL DEFENSE, Daeshik Kim and Tom Leland
LACROSSE FOR GIRLS AND WOMEN, Anne Delano
MODERN DANCE, Esther E. Pease
RACQUETBALL/PADDLEBALL, Philip E. Allsen and Alan Witbeck
PHYSICAL AND PHYSIOLOGICAL CONDITIONING FOR MEN, Benjamin Ricci
RUGBY, J. Gavin Reid
SKIING, Clayne Jensen and Karl Tucker
SKIN AND SCUBA DIVING, Albert A. Tillman
SOCCER, Richard L. Nelson
SOCCER AND SPEEDBALL FOR WOMEN, Jane A. Mott
SOCIAL DANCE, William F. Pillich
SOFTBALL, Marian E. Kneer and Charles L. McCord
SQUASH RACQUETS, Margaret Varner Bloss and Norman Bramall
SWIMMING, Betty J. Vickers and William J. Vincent
SWIMMING, ADVANCED, James A. Gaughran
TABLE TENNIS, Margaret Varner Bloss and J. R. Harrison
TAP DANCE, Barbara Nash
TENNIS, Joan Johnson and Paul Xanthos
TENNIS, ADVANCED, Chet Murphy
TRACK AND FIELD, Kenneth E. Foreman and Virginia L. Husted
TRAMPOLINING, Jeff T. Hennessy
VOLLEYBALL, Glen H. Egstrom and Frances Schaafsma
WEIGHT TRAINING, Philip J. Rasch
WRESTLING, Arnold Umbach and Warren R. Johnson

PHYSICAL EDUCATION
ACTIVITIES SERIES

TRAMPOLINING

JEFF T. HENNESSY

University of Southwestern Louisiana

*Director, 3rd World Trampoline
Championships*

WM. C. BROWN COMPANY PUBLISHERS
DUBUQUE, IOWA

Copyright © 1968 by
Wm. C. Brown Company Publishers

Library of Congress Catalog Card Number: 68-19452

ISBN 0–697–07034–4

Printed in U. S. A.

Preface

With the increased popularity of any activity comes the desire to learn the whys and hows of performance. Unfortunately, many misconceptions and poor, if not dangerous, ideas arise in the absence of good instruction. This book was written to help students learn in a manner which has been proven successful and safe.

Trampolining is a sport on the move. Schools, colleges, universities, and other organizations, such as the AAU, YMCA, YWCA, and Recreation Clubs, now include this activity in their programs. Probably the biggest drawback to success is a lack of knowledge of the sport and the assumption that it is dangerous. This attitude is a direct reflection of lack of knowledge. The purpose of this publication is to:

1. present information based on proper progressions;
2. present activities which can be understood, evaluated, and enjoyed;
3. present skills which are applicable to both men and women;
4. encourage participation in this activity which potentially offers so much satisfaction, enjoyment, and challenge.

Self-evaluation questions are distributed throughout the text. These afford the reader typical examples of the kinds of understandings and skills that he should be acquiring as he progresses in his mastery of the trampoline. The reader should not only answer the printed questions but should pose additional ones as a self check on his learning. These evaluative materials are not always positioned according to the presentation in the text. If the reader finds that he cannot respond fully or accurately to a question, he will need to read more extensively or gain more experience.

v

He can then return to the troublesome questions from time to time until he is sure of the answers or has developed the skill required, as the case may be.

The author acknowledges his debt to all of the youngsters he has known who have participated in the sport of trampolining. The most significant contribution to the realization of this text was made by the author's children, Jeff, Jr., age 10, and Leigh, age 8, and their friend, Tommy Delhomme, age 10. It was these youngsters whose performance motivated this attempt to pass along to others a means by which they, too, might share the enjoyment experienced by Jeff, Leigh, and Tommy. The drawings used in this publication were taken from motion pictures of these three children. A debt of gratitude is extended to Miss Sharon Vanek for the many hours that she spent in preparing these drawings.

Jeff T. Hennessy

Contents

Development
of Trampolining

Trampolining is a rather new activity though it has a long but unrecorded history dating back perhaps to prehistoric man. One can assume that during these early years someone found that by different means he could spring into the air and somersault. The attempt to do so has continued through the years. During the middle ages, man was still trying to fly but continued to have the basic problem of overcoming gravity. This natural phenomenon prevented the best entertainers from doing many skills which they would like to have performed.

Man's imagination and ingenuity, however, was not to be denied. Since many individuals depended upon their ability to perform as a source of livelihood, efforts were made to devise methods of gaining time in the air. One of the first devices for this purpose was the springboard. Another, and more closely associated with trampolining, was called the "leaps"; this was devised by jesters of the royal courts during the middle ages. It consisted of a resilient plank of wood supported well off the floor at both ends by blocks of some type. The jester bounced up and down on the board to perform his skills. Performance on the leaps required considerable skill because the wooden plank was not wide and did not provide a soft landing. Such devices had obvious disadvantages, but improvements were constantly introduced by tumblers and acrobats in an effort to improve their skills and thus to keep the public interested.

Circus performers used a net under the trapeze from which to rebound. One such performer, a Frenchman "du Trampoline," contributed much to the development of the apparatus known today as a trampoline, in particular a system of spring suspensions similar to that now used.

DEVELOPMENT OF TRAMPOLINING

The term *trampolín* is actually a Spanish word meaning "diving board." As used today, the word trampoline, though originally a trade name for the commercial apparatus manufactured by George Nissen, designates the sport itself.

For years, the trampoline was used by theatrical and circus people! These professionals contributed significantly to the sport by developing new skills, by perfecting techniques, and by popularizing the sport through their performances. One such performer was Joe E. Brown who performed a triple back somersault with a full twist on a 4' × 7' trampoline with a canvas bed and elastic shock cords.

The trampoline came into its own with the outbreak of World War II when it was introduced into the recreational and physical education program of the armed forces. It proved to be an efficient means of instructing pilot trainees in many of the body positions and sensations associated with true flight. In addition, it helped in the development of muscular control and coordination, a sharp sense of timing and balance, relocation, and mental and physical confidence, all of which are absolutely essential to flying.

Many physical educators who witnessed the benefits and enjoyment of trampolining in the service programs introduced the activity in the schools throughout the United States upon returning home after the war. This, beginning as early as 1946, led to the development of trampolining as a competitive sport. Today, the trampoline is popular in physical education, as well as in competitive programs and is officially recognized by the NCAA, NAIA, and AAU. With the formation of the International Trampoline Federation and the four World Championships (the first in London in 1964), trampolining has gained international status. Rules for competition may be found in the official rule books of the various governing bodies published annually by the Amateur Athletic Union, National Collegiate Athletic Association, National Association of Intercollegiate Athletics, and the International Trampoline Federation.

2

Body Positions and Mechanics of Trampolining

Before even approaching a trampoline, one must be familiar with the basic body positions and then with the mechanics of trampolining. This information should be studied and then practiced off the trampoline and then on the trampoline until the positions and mechanics become almost automatic. Then effort can be exerted toward greater mastery of the skills of trampolining.

POSITIONS OF THE BODY

There are five basic body positions employed on the trompoline as compared with four on the diving board.

1. In the *tuck* position, the knees are bent and together, hips are flexed, and the hands grasp the legs below the knees. This tuck position, with the body resembling a ball, enables the performer to rotate with great speed around the lateral and dorsoventral axis.

2. The body bent at the waist with the legs straight and together, and hands grasping behind the legs in the area of the knees, is known as the *pike* position. The chest must be reasonably close to the thighs, and the arms which are bent at the elbows are pressed against the sides of the body. Rotation is not as fast in the pike as in the tuck position because speed of rotation increases with the shortening of the body.

A variation where the arms are extended fore sidewards while the body is flexed at the hips and the legs extended is called the "open pike."

3. In the *layout* position, rotation is even slower. Here, the body is straight with no forward bend, rather the position is usually associated with an arched back.

4. The *pucked* position, not used in springboard diving, is used with twisting multiple somersaults. This is an intermediate position between tuck and pike. The hips are flexed and the knees bent, though not completely as in the tuck. The body is more elongated but is not as long as in the pike position where the legs are kept straight. The arms are generally kept in close to the body somewhere in the area of the chest.

5. The fifth or *free* position is used when executing twisting, single, and multiple somersaults, where more than one body position is used in addition to the pucked position. The free position consists of a combination of any two of the four positions, layout, pike, tuck, or pucked. In addition, any of the twisting somersaults are considered free as they may be done in any body position. It is most desirable, however, to do all twisting single somersaults with straight legs.

MECHANICS OF TRAMPOLINING

Beginners should understand the reason why certain things happen. Since trampolining involves the human body, and there are many unknowns involved (personality, fear, desire, judgment, and the like), the following discussion is given in general terms and does not necessarily apply to the application of free-falling dead weight.

The trampoline bed, which is suspended within a metal frame by springs or elastic bands, is set in motion by the downward push of the performer's body weight as he lands. The resulting depression in the bed is directly related to the body weight and the distance it falls before contacting the bed.

When the trampoline bed is depressed at the center, the resulting upward force is perpendicular to the surface. As the performer moves away from the center of the bed and approaches either end, the line of force is toward the center and is no longer perpendicular to the surface. This explains why certain things happen while performing the same skill at different positions on the trampoline.

1. *Body rotation around the lateral axis*

Rotation around the lateral axis (somersaults) involves the controlled application of many mechanical forces. Forward rotation can be accomplished in two different ways, depending on the location of the

4

Evaluation Questions

If you bounce at the end of the trampoline, in which direction will the line of force tend to propel you? Where on the bed is the upward force vertical?

performer on the trampoline bed as he begins and on the desired amount of forward or backward travel, if any, that may be required.

a. If forward rotation with forward travel is desired, this can be accomplished by leaning forward so that the center of gravity of the body is in front of the base and beyond the line of force. As the trampoline bed rebounds and since the center of gravity is forward and outside of the base and in front of the application of force, forward rotation results. Forward travel then is accomplished by pushing backwards with the feet, the amount and angle determining the amount of travel. Knowing how hard to push in order to accomplish the desired amount of travel comes with experience.

Leaning toward the center becomes more pronounced as the ends of the trampoline are approached since the line of force there is not perpendicular to the surface but at an angle toward the center.

On takeoff when the body is straight and upright, rotation around the lateral axis will not occur if the center of gravity is directly above the point of application and follows the line of force created by the rebound of the trampoline bed. This is what occurs when performing the fundamental bounce without rotation.

b. Forward rotation with backward travel is accomplished by keeping the center of gravity within the base. As the trampoline rebounds, the chest must be forward and over the base (feet) while the hips are flexed, are back and behind the base. Here the center of gravity is located outside of the body (as in *a*) but is still directly over the point of application of force which is not the case in *a*.

5

BODY POSITIONS AND MECHANICS

The amount and angle of forward push with the feet determines the amount of backward travel. The more perpendicular the push against the bed, the less will backward travel occur. Backward rotation and travel may be accomplished by applying the same two principles, but in reverse.

In order to perform safely on the trampoline, the student must be aware of these four types of takeoff (two forward and two backward) and know when to use the one most applicable to the situation at hand.

Of interest here is why the student, when performing the fundamental bounce on the ends of the trampoline and facing its center, has the tendency to (1) bounce forward toward the center, (2) bend at the hips to maintain balance, and (3) fall backward if the legs buckle or collapse. The line of force of the trampoline bed, as previously mentioned, is

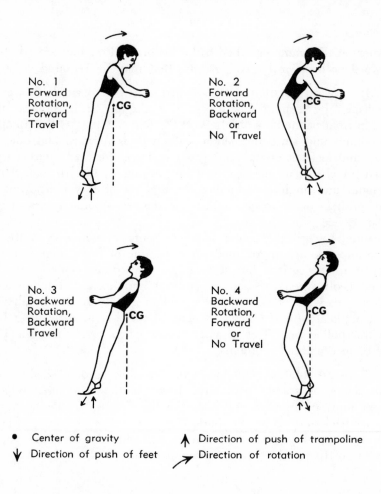

No. 1
Forward
Rotation,
Forward
Travel

No. 2
Forward
Rotation,
Backward
or
No Travel

No. 3
Backward
Rotation,
Backward
Travel

No. 4
Backward
Rotation,
Forward
or
No Travel

•   Center of gravity   ↟   Direction of push of trampoline

↓   Direction of push of feet   ↗   Direction of rotation forward in the direction of the center and tends to become perpendicular at the center. This, therefore, tends to push the feet forward and up causing the student to bounce and travel forward. It also causes him at times to bend over at the hips in a slight pike position while in the air in order to counter the lifting of the feet in front and to maintain balance. This same line of force causes backward rotation when his legs buckle or collapse under him.

In order to overcome this line of force near either end of the trampoline, it is necesary to try to remain perpendicular to the surface of the trampoline and to push away from the line of force at the point of application. The resulting action then is a controlled bounce perpendicular to the bed.

2. *Body rotation around the longitudinal axis*

Rotation around the longitudinal axis (twisting) is initiated while still in contact with the bed in most cases. Twisting in a single somersault begins while the feet are still in contact with the bed. This is not necessarily true, however, when more than one somersault is done and the twist is in the last somersault.

Twisting also may be started while free in the air by swinging the arms and turning the head and shoulders in the desired direction of the twist, provided there is angular motion. Here, the performer takes advantage of gravity, and twisting is easiest as the body approaches the horizontal position.

When the body is in flight and perpendicular and there is no angular motion, twisting is of the action-reaction type. This is accomplished by swinging the arms in the opposite direction of the desired twist. Stand on a round rotary-type piano stool and try this; the results of the application of this principle are clear.

3

For All Performers

There are some basic factors to consider in the use of a trampoline. These are necessary for individual use of the trampoline and for teaching use of the trampoline.

SAFETY

It is quite easy to lose sight of the potential danger of injury while bouncing on the trampoline. The trampoline is probably no more hazardous than many other physical activities, but it offers such challenge that a performer can become carried away with his success. For this reason, it is important that this activity be supervised *at all times*; the trampoline *should never* be used unless the instructor is present. The equipment should be kept locked and should not be used before, between, or after class without supervision. Participants must not perform without proper spotters, at least one on each end and one on each side, and no somersaulting action should ever be attempted before appropriate progressions have been mastered.

When one first mounts the trampoline, he will be told merely to climb up and climb down. (Without this explicit direction, many beginners will jump from the trampoline to the floor, and this could result in injury.) He will be cautioned to watch a specific spot on the trampoline while jumping and not to jump too high. Control of position on the trampoline is most important; the student must watch the trampoline so that he will not lose his sense of balance and fall.

Evaluation Questions

Do you know the safe thing to do under these circumstances:
a. while bouncing, you lose your balance backwards;
b. two friends offer to spot while you practice;
c. a classmate wants to stand on the tramp bed while you bounce;
d. you are ready to dismount?

As one gains experience, he will develop control and confidence. This, coupled with good safety procedures, will lead to many hours of enjoyable trampolining.

Following are some common safety regulations which should be *adhered to implicitly.*

1. The trampoline should never be left unsupervised.
2. The trampoline should be kept locked when not in use.
3. Street shoes should not be worn on the trampoline.
4. Safety pads on the frame of the trampoline should be provided.
5. Only a trampoline in good condition should ever be used.
6. There should be an adequate number of trained spotters.
7. Use proper spotting equipment when needed.
8. While spotting, the spotter should never rest the hands and arms on the suspension system as an arm may be broken should the performer on the trampoline fall.
9. Be alert while spotting—watch the student who is jumping.
10. The student should learn means by which to prevent unnecessary minor injuries. He should learn what not to do as well as what to do.
11. Make a habit of always climbing up and down the trampoline.
12. To prevent loss of control, bounce for short periods of time only.
13. Know your limitations but have confidence.
14. Never attempt skills when fatigued.
15. Never engage in indiscriminate bouncing.
16. Never stagger backward to regain your balance. Sit down so that you will not stagger off the end of the trampoline.
17. Never should more than one student be on the trampoline at one time.

18. Proper learning progression must be closely followed.
19. Horse play should not be tolerated.

ORGANIZATION

Since not more than one should bounce on the trampoline at one time, the class will be organized so that the available time will be best utilized by all. Normally, trampolining is one of several activities included in a gymnastic or sports unit. In this case, the squad system probably will be utilized so that the number of students involved in each activity is reduced to a workable size. These squads usually rotate from one activity to another during the class period.

If this is not the case and only trampolining is being taught, the group should be limited to no more than ten per trampoline. If more than one trampoline is used, they will be placed side by side about four to five feet apart.

During the instructional part of the period, the students should be stationed around all four sides of the trampoline to act as spotters as well as to observe the demonstration of skills to be learned.

During the first class session, the students will probably be given the following:

1. A short history of the trampoline.
2. The name and an explanation of the parts of the equipment.
3. An idea of the cost of the various parts of the unit and the necessity of taking care of the trampoline and keeping it in good working order.
4. A demonstration of how to fold and unfold the trampoline so that the equipment will not be damaged and so that no injuries will occur to the students.
5. Experience in folding and unfolding the trampoline.
6. The basic safety rules and reasons for their enforcement.
7. A demonstration of how to mount, how to do the fundamental bounce, and then how to dismount.
8. Experience in following this procedure.

The fundamental skills must be mastered and confidence developed so that all can perform with poise. New skills will be kept at a minimum height so that good control will be developed. During succeeding sessions, the student will be instructed in proper progressions. The number of new skills presented will depend on ability.

4

Basic
Spotting Procedures

Spotting, or guarding the performer, is an art that must be learned, cultivated, and unfailingly practiced. The function of spotters is to prevent the person on the trampoline from falling on the floor. The spotter must push this person back onto the trampoline and should not try to catch him in flight. This may sound like a simple task, but a spotter without experience tends to back off from a free-falling body because it presents a picture of danger and possible injury.

There must be a sense of cooperation between the spotter and the performer. The performer must have confidence in his spotters, and he must, at all times, endeavor to finish the skill that he sets out to do. This practice serves two ends—it presents a better target for the spotter to push against, and a performer is less likely to be injured if he finishes what he starts out to do.

Spotting from bed level takes practice. The spotter must keep time with the bed so that he does not interfere with the rhythm of the performance in progress. By placing one foot on the frame and one on the bed, the foot on the bed can be lifted when the bed is depressed by the individual performing and replaced when the bed rebounds. In this way, the spotter can step onto the bed when needed. Knowing when he is needed and assisting accordingly requires split-second timing.

Another type of on-bed spotting requires the spotter (often the instructor) to bounce with the learner. When the performer's feet leave the bed, the spotter's do not. He "gives" with the up action so that he does not interfere but depresses the bed as the student lands thus giving him

11

a mild double bounce. While this procedure is being used, the spotter can keep his hands on the student at all times, if necessary.

The use of the safety belt both on and off the trampoline is most important. Two people can support a performer with a safety belt and short lengths of rope by using the method of one foot on the frame and the other on the bed. As a new skill is performed, both spotters step onto the bed and lift up. It is not advisable to try skills involving more than one somersault for it is difficult to support a falling body from the height necesary to complete two somersaults.

Twisting skills can be learned with or without a twisting belt. If a twisting belt is not available, simply wrap the ropes around the waist in the opposite direction from that in which the twist is to be done and pull the ropes as the somersaulting action is done. With this system, the spotters actually spin the performer around.

Finally, spotting can be achieved from an overhead device, suspended from a beam, consisting of one single and one double pulley, a length of rope, and a belt. The pulleys should be far enough apart so that the rope will not interfere with the arm action in twisting. The trampoline should be centered on the floor halfway between the two pulleys. The spotter stands to the side of the trampoline and pulls down on the rope when the performer springs up and lets out on the rope when he drops to the bed. In this fashion, the spotter can keep time with the up-and-down action, keeping the ropes out of the way, and at the same time sustaining maximum control over the actions of the learner.

As skill develops, less and less support is given by the spotter until no help is given at all. At this point, the student will be encouraged to initiate the skill without a belt. The spotter should then assume a position of on-bed spotting to protect the student as he attempts the skill for the first time without the belt. A certain amount of fear is natural when there no longer is outside help; this fear is lessened by the presence of the spotter standing on the frame of the trampoline.

The next day when the new skill is again attempted, it is wise to do it in the belt a few times in order to regain the "feel" before performing without support.

5

Basic Skills
for the Beginner

All the basic skills discussed in this chapter originate from the fundamental bounce. The bounce precedes the performance of each. All twisting skills are described from right to left.

FUNDAMENTAL BOUNCE

To execute the fundamental bounce, the performer starts from a standing position with chest up, arms by his sides, head in a normal position, and eyes fixed on a point somewhere on the bed of the trampoline in front of him. His feet should be about 12 inches apart and in line, with heels level with the trampoline bed but with the body weight forward on the balls of the feet. Movement is started by lifting the arms side upwards to a point just above the head while pressing up onto the toes. This action causes the bed to be set into motion. As the arms are swung down (back to front), the knees are flexed and the heels drop down to the level of the trampoline. This movement causes the bed to be depressed. When the arms reach their lowest point, they are swung up in a more frontal position and the legs are extended causing a further depression of the bed. On reaching the maximum depression, the legs should be completely extended and ready for the upward push from the trampoline bed. Lift-off should be with ankle extension and as the student becomes airborne, he should press his legs together. If the legs are not extended on takeoff, the end result is the uncontrolled collapse of the student's legs.

The drop is made in a perpendicular plane with the surface of the trampoline bed, with the legs spread about 12 inches just prior to landing on the feet. The knees and hips are slightly flexed when the landing is made to take up the landing shock, with the first contact being made with the balls of the feet. The arms swing down from back to front and are below shoulder height on landing. As the trampoline is further depressed, the heels drop down onto the bed and the legs cease to give as the full weight settles on the bed. As maximum depression is approached, the legs and hips extend and push downward causing a further depression. The arms continue their downward swing and should reach their lowest point when maximum depression is reached. On recoil, the knees and hips continue to extend and push the body upward. As this upward motion begins, the arms continue the circle and swing upward in a more frontal position. This arm action helps body balance; it also supplies a further force in depressing the trampoline and lifting the body on takeoff.

Bouncing on the trampoline can be compared with that on the springboard during the hurdle and takeoff. There is, however, one basic difference—the arms are not fully extended over the head on each jump. The height of the arms over the head depends on the individual performing

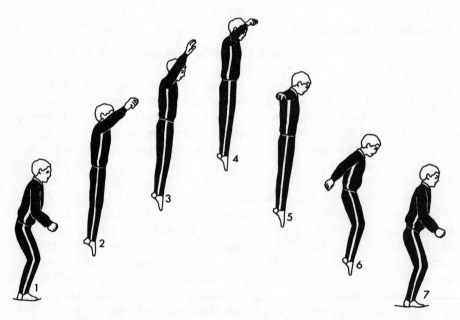

Figure 1—Fundamental Bounce and Kill the Bounce

the fundamental jump, but the arms should be well extended in the direction of takeoff when a skill other than the fundamental jump is performed. The performer should sight some spot on the trampoline while jumping and never close his eyes. Landings should be made as close to the point of departure as possible, thus minimizing travel. This principle should be applied to the performance of all skills.

KILL THE BOUNCE

This must be learned by every beginner so that he can stop bouncing without losing control. One simply should flex the hips and knees on landing and not push down on the trampoline bed with the feet. By doing this, he will absorb the rebounding action.

CHANGE OF DIRECTION (twist is to the left from the bed)

A simple means of changing direction while doing the fundamental bounce should be learned next. While jumping on the feet, twisting action is started before lift-off by pushing down and to the right with both

Figure 2—Change of Direction from the Bed

Can you change direction 1/4 turn on each successive bounce? 1/2 turn? one full turn? Can you do these turns both to the right and to the left?

Evaluation Questions

feet in order to twist left. As the body lifts, the shoulders, head, and arms turn left; the performer then executes a one-half twist before landing. More than one-half twist may be accomplished if one is more vigorous with the twisting action.

CHANGE OF DIRECTION (twist to the left while in the air)

This type of twisting has limited value, but it does teach the individual how to correct an error prior to landing thus preventing possible injury.

While airborne during a fundamental jump, he swings the right arm, head, and shoulder to the right and the hips to the left. As the hips turn left, he will push the left arm across the stomach and to the right. This action-reaction motion will result in a twist left.

SEAT DROP OR SEAT BOUNCE

From a low fundamental bounce, the performer lifts the legs from the hips to a sitting position, with knees extended. The landing is at the same point as the takeoff (little or no travel); the seat, legs, hands, and heels should come into contact with the bed at the same time. The upper body should be leaning back slightly to prevent forward bending at the hips. The latter could result in an injury to the face caused by striking the knees. Both hands, the fingers pointing forward, should land on the bed behind and to the side of the hips. The head and chest are in a normal sitting position. To regain the feet, one must push with the hands

Figure 3—Change of Direction in the Air

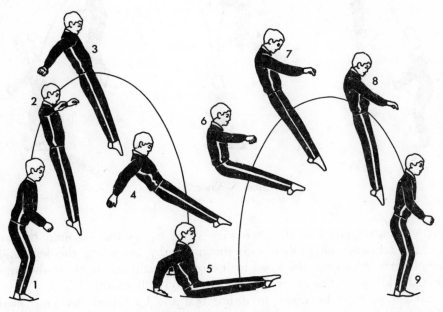

Figure 4—Seat Drop

lifting the chest and hips up and press the legs and feet down to a standing position. When control is developed, the height of the performance can be increased.

KNEE DROP OR KNEE BOUNCE

From the fundamental bounce, the performer lands on the knees, shins, and instep simultaneously. The body is kept rigid from the knees up, with no flexion at the hips. He will keep the head erect with eyes fixed on the trampoline in front of him. As the drop is made, the arms swing down as

Figure 5—Knee Drop

in the fundamental bounce; then they swing up as the rebound begins. On the rebound, he pushes with the instep by extending the legs and keeping the hips over the knee to insure a straight-up flight. If the hips drop back behind the knees, backward motion will result.

Caution must be taken to insure that the back and neck are held rigid in order to prevent whiplash when the bed rebounds.

HANDS AND KNEE DROP OR HANDS AND KNEE BOUNCE

The hands and knee drop is similar to the knee drop except that landing is made on the hands and knees simultaneously. The position is much like that of crawling. This skill is a prerequisite to the front drop.

From a moderate amount of height, the performer bends forward at the hips keeping the back parallel with the surface of the trampoline and the knees flexed. At the same time, he extends the arm down and locks the elbows, thus making it possible to land on the knees and hands simultaneously. The hips are over the knees, and the shoulders are over the hands. On landing, the head is held up and the arms are partially bent at the elbows in order to absorb some of the force upon impact. Care must be taken not to relax or one will find his face buried in the trampoline bed. To return to original starting position, he will push with the hands, lift the chest, and pull the legs down to a standing position.

Figure 6—Hands and Knee Drop

FRONT DROP OR FRONT BOUNCE

To perform the front drop properly, one must keep in mind that the trampoline is not a diving board, and the intention is not to do a front

How can this stomach landing be corrected?

Evaluation Questions

FRONT DROP

dive. Many with springboard diving experience dive forward when first attempting the front drop. Keep in mind that no forward travel is needed. Begin with the same bending action as in the hands and knee drop. The performer will raise his head and extend his legs prior to dropping to the bed.

Figure 7—Front Drop

Diagram A:

FRONT DROP

Contact is made with a slight arch in the back and with the knees bent about 90°. When the landing is made, weight is distributed from the knees to about halfway up the rib cage. The upper part of the chest and head do not contact the bed. The neck is rigid with the face forward and head up while the shoulders and upper chest are supported by the forearm with elbows bent and away from the body. The hands are placed palms down and in the area of the face. The landing must be flat or injury to the back or neck might occur as well as abrasions to the body. To regain the feet, push with the hands, lift the chest up, pull the legs down and forward with the hips flexed to a standing position.

BACK DROP OR BACK BOUNCE

Though the back drop is not too difficult, there is a definite reason for placing it last in basic landing positions. This skill is "blind"—the performer cannot see the landing as has been the case with the previous skills.

From a stand, one will fall backwards lifting the legs, land flat on the back from the hips to the shoulders, with the chin tucked forward and down. It is not wise to start this skill from a bounce because frequently the landing is made on the hips, and this causes the head to be snapped back with discomfort. A good landing is flat on the back with legs flexed at the knees at about a 45° angle with the trampoline. As the landing improves, the height from which the skill is performed should be increased.

The "kip" is used to rebound the performer from his back to his feet. He must extend the legs up, forward, then down while the back of the

What will happen in the tuck jump if you drop your head and chest to meet your legs? if you lean backward as you lift your legs? if you hold your legs too long?

Evaluation Questions

shoulders push against the bed as the arms swing forward to activate a lifting and forward rotating action. As the chest is lifted, the legs are swung down for a landing on the feet.

Figure 8—Back Drop

TUCK JUMP

Starting from a jump, the legs are lifted up by flexing the hips; pulling the legs up to the chest puts the performer in a ball or tuck position. He grasps the legs just below the knees to complete the tuck. The head and chest are held erect with the chin tucked and eyes looking down.

If he drops his head and chest down to meet the legs instead of pulling the legs up to the chest, he will topple over forward and lose his balance. By the same token, one does not lean backward when the legs are lifted and does not hold on to the legs for too long. Holding the legs too long makes it difficult to extend the legs for a proper landing.

Figure 9—Tuck Jump

STRADDLE JUMP

A straddle jump begins from a bounce with the legs being lifted up and spread as the performer becomes airborne. The hips are flexed with legs spread fore sideways and extended in what could be described as a straddle sitting position in the air. The arms reach out fore sideways so

Do you know two of the errors that prevent success in the swivel hips? Do you know three errors? four errors?

Evaluation Questions

that the hands touch the instep of both feet simultaneously. One must not bend over too far to meet the legs on the way up or balance will be lost. The best system is to place the hands in a position lower than the shoulders and try to kick them with the feet. If the hands are too high, the legs will be lifted too high and the performer will fall backwards.

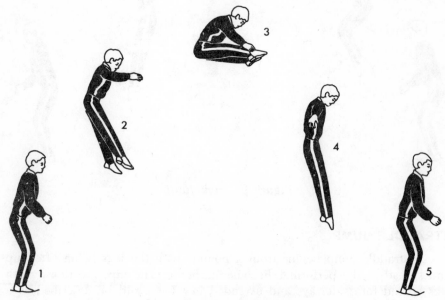

Figure 10—Straddle Jump

After the touch is made, the legs swing down, the arms swing up, and the chest is lifted in preparation for landing on the feet.

SWIVEL HIPS (twist is to the left)

From a seat drop landing, the hands push downward and to the right causing the shoulders to turn left with the head. On lift-off, the performer swings the arms up over his head, swings the legs down and directly under as the chest is lifted. When a standing position is reached, the hands should be overhead with a one-quarter twist completed. The head continues its left turn as the arms and shoulders swing left around and forward to complete the half twist. The hips are flexed and a seat drop completes the skill. What is accomplished is a seat drop, one-half twist, seat drop.

Generally, there are four errors that prevent completion of this skill on the first few tries. These are:

1. Jumping forward when doing the seat drop
2. Landing with legs up off the bed on the seat drop
3. Trying to swing the legs around to the side when twisting
4. Failure to swing the arms up over the head while twisting

Figure 11—Swivel Hips

CRADLE

The cradle is actually a swivel hip from a back drop. After landing on the back, kip (refer to back drop) forward and up beginning a half turn left on lift-off. The arms are then swung left up over the head and the legs come down and directly under the body as the chest is lifted. When in an upright position, the hands should be overhead with the head turned left. The one-half twist is completed at this point, and the skill is completed with a back drop.

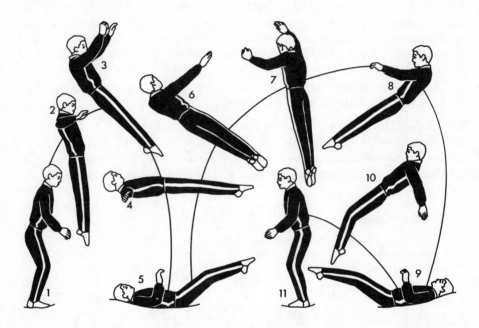

Figure 12—Cradle

The twisting action can be delayed if desired so that the twist is completed just prior to landing on the back.

SWINGTIME AND ADD-ONE

Doing one skill right after the other with no free bounce between is "swingtime." Swingtime can best be mastered by the game of "add-one."

Add-one is a low-level type of competition where a performer must do what the preceding student did and then add on a skill. Each landing terminates a skill and the next skill must be done from the last landing position. The game should be confined to the level of skills learned in class. When a participant is unable to perform the routine when his turn comes up, he is eliminated from the game. This procedure is followed until a winner is declared. The order of competition of the first game is by a draw, but each succeeding game is determined by the order of placement of the preceding game. For example, the winner goes first, second place goes second, and so on.

FORM

Form is a necessary part of trampolining. In order to perform with precision and finesse, it is important for an individual to be constantly aware of his form. It is much easier to execute a skill without form than with it. Form is important but only after a skill is learned. If the student must worry about form while learning, then learning becomes difficult.

Generally speaking, form is the appearance given during a performance, and this depends on the way that the skills are executed. Appearance should be appealing, presenting a picture of grace and beauty. To accomplish this, the body must be kept as streamlined as possible. No unnecessary movement should detract from the performance as a whole. The fingers should be extended and together; feet should be together with toes pointed. In piked and layout positions, the legs should be together and extended until just prior to landing. Each movement should have a purpose and must be done in such a way as to present a picture of smooth continuity.

LANDING ON THE FEET AND TAKEOFF

The landing on the feet is important for it affects the learning and performance of all skills. If poor landing habits are developed, the takeoff and execution of succeeding skills will be affected when performed in swingtime. The landing should be made with hips flexed, chest over the feet, with legs bent at the knees. This allows for a longer stay in the trampoline bed, and this results in better control and lift. Hands and arms should be somewhere between the waist and shoulders in a fore sideway position. If the arms are above the shoulders on landing, the landing is poor and, in most cases, indicates over-rotation. For stability, the feet should be about twelve inches apart and in line, with eyes fixed on the spot of contact.

As the performer settles into the bed, the chest is lifted upright with legs flexed at the knees. The head is lifted to an upright or normal position with the eyes still on some spot on the bed. As the arms swing up, the legs are extended, and the performer is lifted with a maximum of thrust for the next skill. One should always attempt to land as close to the point of departure as possible. A beginner should not lean while learning a skill because he is not aware of just how much lean is safe.

ADDITIONAL BASIC BEGINNER SKILLS

There are many more skills that fall under the heading of basic beginner skills. Some have more than one landing and are, therefore, combinations rather than single skills. The vast number makes it impossible to analyze each one. The names of several, however, will give some indication of the method of execution.

1. Fundamental bounce with full twist
2. Pike jump
3. Seat drop, full twist, seat drop (twist in sitting position)
4. Back drop, full twist, back drop (twist in back drop position)
5. Front drop with one-half twist to back
6. Front drop with one twist to stomach
7. Back drop with one-half twist to stomach
8. Back drop with one twist to back (twist before or after landing)
9. Back drop, one-half twist to feet
10. Seat drop, one-half twist to feet
11. Back drop, one-half front somersault to front drop
12. Front drop, one-half back somersault to back drop
13. Front drop, one-half somersault sideways to front drop (one-half turn table)
14. Front drop, one somersault sideways to front drop (full turn table)
15. Seat drop, one-quarter front somersault to stomach drop
16. Game of add-one

Basic
Intermediate Skills

Basic intermediate skills, being more advanced, will require more time to master. These are divided here into three categories—beginner intermediate, intermediate, and advanced intermediate. Each category is directly related to the other and provides a logical order of progression. It would be foolish to undertake the execution of some of the more advanced skills without first mastering their prerequisites.

BEGINNER INTERMEDIATE SKILLS

Front Somersault (tuck)

Stand facing the center of the trampoline about two feet from the end and execute a front roll from a squatting position. Repeat the front roll several times, becoming aware of relative body position. Now, perform the front roll with a slight bounce without using your hands. There is no need for a high bounce, but your hands should be in a position to catch you if necessary.

Following the same procedure, bounce higher and execute a three-quarter front somersault to the back. Then go on to perform the three-quarter front somersault to the seat. The final phase is to the feet. This is the logical order of progression to follow while learning the front somersault. Since there is more to it than this, however, you should know what happens when a somersault is attempted so that you can correct your errors.

The front somersault begins with a push of the feet on the trampoline. The head, chest, and arms lead the way up and forward as you bend at the hips. This bending at the hips tends to stabilize the center of gravity over the point of departure. (Refer to Chapter 2.)

As your arms reach up, the hips are lifted, the feet are pressed up and backward toward the buttocks as you bend at the hips and flex the legs at the knees. When the hips and knees are flexed, swing the arms down forcefully and tuck the chin down to increase the forward speed of rotation. Your hands grasp the legs just below the knees with elbows in close to the body, and the chest is pulled down to the legs in the direction of the rotation. This action of "going after the legs" is called "chasing the legs." When you approach the sitting down position, the legs are released by allowing them to slide out of the hands. They are extended in a piked position. The legs then swing down to achieve an upright landing position.

Figure 13—Front Somersault

You should see the trampoline on the start and finish of the front somersault but not during it, provided your head is in the proper position and your eyes are open. If trouble develops while attempting to learn the front somersault from the feet, then try it from the hands and knee drop. Caution should be taken not to let the arms bend too much; if they do bend too much, the head will strike the bed when the somersault is started.

Hand Spotting the Front Somersault

The performer stands with his left side to the spotter (the instructor) and both stand on the trampoline. He grasps the right side of the performer's neck and shoulder with his left hand so that the forearm rests on the left shoulder and the thumb is on the right scapula. Both work the

Figure 14—Hand Spotting the Front Somersault

bed together with the performer's feet leaving the bed while the spotter's feet remain in contact at all times but in rhythm so as not to interrupt the performance.

When the somersault begins on a prearranged count, the left arm of the spotter moves in the direction of rotation and acts as a support around which the body rotates. If the somersault action should stall at any point and additional help is needed, the spotter quickly reaches in with his

How can this tuck position be improved?

Evaluation Questions
TUCK POSITION

free hand (in this case, the right hand) placing it somewhere between the middle of the thigh and the center of the chest and pushes in the direction of rotation. This spotting procedure may be reversed for those who perform better with the right arm as the pivot arm.

Back Somersault (tuck)

Standing with your back to the center of the trampoline and about two feet from the end, execute a back roll from a squat, then from a stand. Follow this with the back over which is a three-quarter back somersault from a back takeoff to the feet. Starting with a slight bounce, land on the back with legs high, knees bent, and hips flexed. Roll out of the trampoline bed backward doing a high back roll grasping the knees and lifting off of the bed to a landing on the feet.

Quite often, when first learning, you will not generate enough back rotation to land on your feet. When this occurs, the hands are placed on the mat the same as in the back roll to insure a safe landing on the feet. The next step is the back somersault which will need a hand spot or support in a safety belt, whichever the instructor deems necessary.

A backward somersault begins with a push of the feet against the trampoline. As this action is started, the back is arched and the hips are lifted upward. The arms swing up and over the head, the hips are lifted, then flexed while the legs follow bent at the knees. As the legs are brought up to the body, they are grasped just below the knees and pulled in the direction of rotation. At about the same time that the grasp is made by the hands, the head drops back to sight the bed for

Diagram B:
TUCK POSITION

the landing. At about the three-quarter back somersault position, the legs are released in preparation for landing. On landing, the arms are fore sideways and below your shoulders. If they are above the shoulders, this indicates that too much somersault was done.

Figure 15—Back Somersault Tuck

While learning the back somersault, very few performers will tuck up tightly so will tend to do the skill semi-layout; this is all right but should be discontinued later in favor of the tuck position. The technique of back rotation is basically the same regardless of body position.

Hand Spotting the Back Somersault

The spotter assumes a position to the performer's right on the trampoline. With the left hand, the spotter grasps the back of the performer's neck and with the right hand the performer's pants at the waist. The spotter works the bed up and down with the performer until ready to execute the back somersault on a prearranged count. At this point, the left hand supports the body while the right hand lifts the performer's hips in the direction of rotation. Both hands of the spotter remain on the performer throughout the entire somersault. As the spotter feels less weight and finds that he must do less work to help complete the somersault, he will introduce a change in spotting technique.

Standing with the right foot on the frame and the left foot on the bed, the spotter lifts his left foot each time the performer lands on the bed and replaces it while he is in the air. This enables him to be close at

Figure 16-1—Hand Spotting the Back Somersault

hand and yet not interefere with any movement of the performer. When the somersault is started, the spotter then will step on the bed, reach out with his left hand and place it on the performer's back in the area of the hips to give him support. This type of handspot is continued until the somersault becomes stable. Spotting may be done from either side.

Figure 16-2—Hand Spotting the Back Somersault

Barani (twist is right to left)

The barani is the first twisting somersault action taught and it plays a large role in the learning of many other twisting skills. It is important to learn to twist the same direction in all twisting skills.

The barani is deceiving in looks and feel in relation to the direction of the twist, and sometimes the performer thinks he is twisting one way while actually twisting in the opposite. To determine the direction of the twist, stand to the right side of a performer and have him perform a barani (or round-off if he cannot barani). If you view his back, he is twisting left; if his stomach is seen, he is twisting right. It would work out the same if the performer simply turned left or right while standing upright.

There are several approaches to learning the barani; two are discussed below.

Method 1. Standing facing the center of the trampoline, do a round-off (cart wheel with one-half twist, instead of the usual one-quarter twist). This will place you facing in the opposite direction from which you started. Do several round-offs and be sure that the twist is left. From a low bounce, do the round-off but do not place too much weight on the hands. Continue with this until it is not necessary to place the hands on the trampoline. The final result is a barani.

Method 2. From a knee drop, round-off to the left landing on your knees. Repeat this move but put less weight on your hands. As less weight is applied to the hands, you will find that you are doing a barani from knee drop to knee drop. Next, perform it from knee drop to feet, then feet to feet.

Barani action is introduced with a front somersault and eyes fixed on some spot on the bed in front and usually close to the feet. Both arms lead the way up together as the hips flex and the feet are pressed up behind. As the bending of the hips increases, the arms are swung

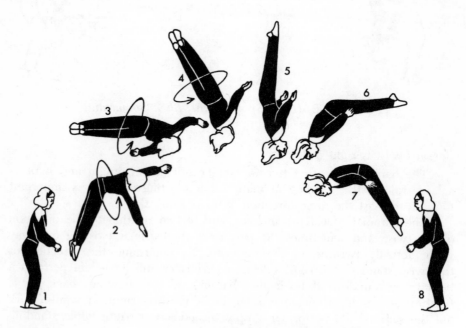

Figure 17—Barani

36

down forcefully in front. The right arm drifts to the right and back while the left arm moves right across the lower chest. Your head is erect with eyes on the trampoline and turned left with the forceful rotation of the shoulders. It would appear that the body twists in the opposite direction as that of the arm swing. Arm flexion at the elbow will vary with each performer. As you reach an upside-down position, the hips are extended and the twist is completed in a predominantly layout position. At this point, the hips are flexed to bring the legs and feet down and under for a landing. During the entire action, hold your head up so that your eyes can view the trampoline.

One peculiar aspect of this particular skill is that there is no sensation of twisting as such but is more of a swivel type action initiated by the hips. Quite frequently, the feeling on completion of the somersault will be of over-twisting when actually not enough twist has been done. If you land with the right arm back to the right and the left arm right across the chest, under-twisting is the correct diagnosis. A proper landing would be with both arms fore sideways and below shoulder level. Though under-twisting, the feeling by the performer will be of over-twisting, and this is a natural feeling because the arms appear to be moving away from the direction of the twist and quite naturally will swing to the right on landing if not corrected before the landing is made.

Spotting the Barani

There are several methods used in the spotting of a barani but by using the proper sequence outlined in this section, there is little need to use a hand spot with this particular skill. If spotting is a last resort to learning the barani, then use a twisting belt for support.

Additional Beginner Intermediate Skills

1. Front one and one-quarter somersault
2. Back one and one-quarter somersault to the seat
3. Back one and one-quarter somersault to the back
4. Front somersault from the seat
5. Front somersault from the knees
6. Back somersault from the knees
7. Ball out (front somersault action from the back drop position)
8. Back somersaults in swingtime
9. Performance of skills in different body positions (tuck, pike, etc.)
10. Combinations of beginner intermediate skills
11. Game of add-one

How can the arm action be improved to increase the speed of the twist?

INTERMEDIATE SKILLS

Three-quarter Back Somersault

It is a little more difficult to do less than one somersault backward and land on the stomach than to do the complete somersault and land on the feet. Backward rotating skills to the stomach could lead to discomfort for the performer and therefore should be discussed and analyzed by the performer and the instructor before these skills are attempted. An individual must be able to perform the back somersault with complete confidence and be able to visually sight the trampoline bed long before landing. In essence, the three-quarter back somersault is a slow back somersault with the landing on the stomach.

This skill should first be done with the legs bent to attain better control. When the eyes sight the bed, the body is extended for a somach landing. When one becomes more confident, less bending is needed until the skill is done layout. When learning, if the three-quarter is overturned, land on the knees or feet; if under-turned, land on the hands and knees. It all goes back to the fact that one must be able to see his landing in order to correct any errors that may occur.

The landing is made with the head back, back arched, and legs flexed at the knees. This flexion of the knees should occur just prior to the landing and not during the three-quarter back somersault. As the performer comes to rest on the bed, the weight is distributed from the knees to about half-way up the chest. He keeps his neck locked with face forward and head up while the shoulders and upper chest are supported by the forearms with elbows bent and away from the body. The palms of

Diagram C:
TWISTING

the hands are in contact with the bed with hands under the face. To gain his feet, he pushes with his hands in order to lift the chest, and he pulls the legs down by flexing the hips.

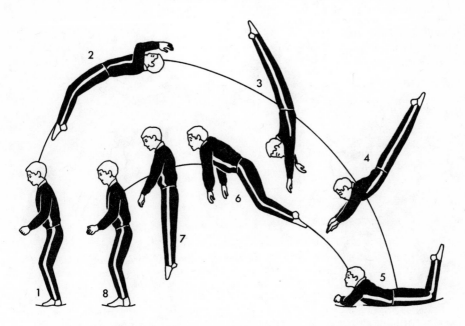

Figure 18—Three-Quarter Back Somersault

39

Back Cody (tuck)

The back cody is a backward rotating somersault from the stomach. The most common type begins from the stomach, and after completing one and one-quarter back somersaults, a landing is made on the feet. Generally, this is accepted as a "back cody."

The back cody begins from a stomach landing after completion of a three-quarter back somersault and *not* from a front drop. It is quite difficult to perform a back cody from a front drop, not that it cannot be done, but it is not likely that the beginner will find it easy to do. From the stomach landing with the knees bent and locked prior to landing, the backward rotating force is started by pushing with the hands against the bed and with the legs in the area of the thighs close to the knees. When this pushing action is combined with the lifting action of the trampoline bed, the performer is lifted off of the bed with the legs extended, then flexed again, whipped under, through, and forward to meet the hands in a backward somersault. His head is back during the backward rotation until his eyes sight the bed for the landing. As the backward rotation is completed, the head begins to drop down. When the

Figure 19—Back Cody Tuck

feet are placed on the bed, the performer's chin should be down with eyes still on the bed. If his head is kept back until the feet are placed on the trampoline, he will look through his landing and be viewing the ceiling in front. When this occurs, the back cody has been over-turned.

Spotting the Back Cody

The spotter steps on to the bed from the side of the trampoline after the cody somersault has started and assists by placing his hands on the upper back and seat, lifting, and pushing in the direction of the rotation.

Figure 20—Spotting the Back Cody

Front Cody (tuck)

The front cody is a forward rotating somersault from the stomach. Starting from a front drop landing, the head is ducked and the arms pulled down and under the chest as the body lifts up out of the bed. The legs remain flexed at the knees as the hips are flexed and lifted up by a push of the legs. The hands and chest continue to move in the direction of the legs thus causing the performer to rotate forward. The

41

Evaluation Questions

hands grasp the legs just below the knees. On completion of about one-
half somersault the legs are released, and a landing is made on the feet
thereby completing the three-quarter somersault or front cody.

Figure 21—Front Cody

Spotting the Front Cody

The spotter stands on the bed with the performer and bounces with him without leaving the bed. When the front drop is made, the spotter helps depress the bed giving a mild double spring for additional height. When the front cody starts, the spotter places one hand on the back and the other on the thigh of the performer and lifts and pushes in the direction of the rotation.

Figure 22—Spotting the Front Cody

Back Somersault, One-Half Twist (twist from right to left)

This skill is a lead-up to the full twisting back somersault and so should be mastered before that somersault is attempted. Starting with an upward swing of both arms as in a back somersault semi-layout, the performer looks back for the trampoline bed. The left arm and shoulder is pushed left while the right arm continues upward. At about one-half somersault or later, the twist starts and the eyes are fixed on the trampoline bed. As the twist continues left, the head remains stationary and does not turn. This causes the performer to be looking over the right shoulder as the twist approaches its completion. In addition, the left arm

43

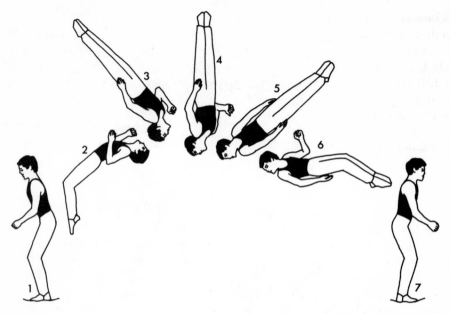

Figure 23-1—Back Somersault, One-Half Twist

Figure 23-2—Three-Quarter Back Somersault, One-Half Twist

is brought down and across the front of the performer's body about waist high and the right arm drops down in line with the body.

Prior to completion of the somersault, the performer turns his head left to face front, the left arm swings left to the side and the right arm is lifted to the right. Both arms should be below shoulder level and extended to the sides. At this point, the landing is made on the feet. This process should be repeated many times with efforts made to twist earlier because this leads to a full twisting back somersault. To complete the twist, one's head, arms, and shoulders must all move in the same direction which in this case is from right to left.

Full Twisting Back Somersault (twist right to left)

Twisting backward begins with a back somersault layout. The back is arched and the hips thrust forward and up. This action tends to keep the performer's center of gravity over the point of takeoff. As the hips are lifted, the feet are pressed up. Both arms lead the way up, the left arm being flexed at the elbow and pressed back, with the right arm above the head. The head is forcefully rotated left with the eyes looking over the left shoulder for the trampoline bed. As the head turns left,

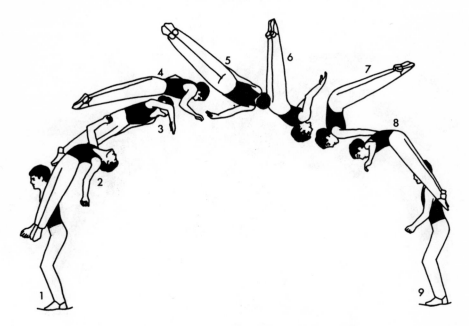

Figure 24—Full Twisting Back Somersault

the right arm swings in the same direction around the head and across the chest. Both shoulders move in the same direction as the arms; otherwise, there will be no twist, only the sensation of twisting.

Termination of the twist is marked with a bending of the hips in a pike position and the arms extended fore sideways and eyes on the bed. After a time, the student will find that the trampoline bed can be seen throughout the performance of this skill. Look for it—it is important to develop a habit of watching the trampoline.

Spotting the full twisting back somersault can be done by hand but should not be necessary when the above procedure is followed; however, should it become necessary, the reader can refer to the chapter on Spotting.

Full Twisting Front Somersault (twist right to left)

The barani can be used as a lead-up to a full twisting front somersault. Upon completion of the barani, the head, shoulders, and arms must continue around in the direction of the twist. In this case, it would be left to complete the 360° circle. There is often a tendency to barani left (one-half twist), then right one-half twist in an attempt to complete the full twist. This is not a complete twist left but has the feel of a full

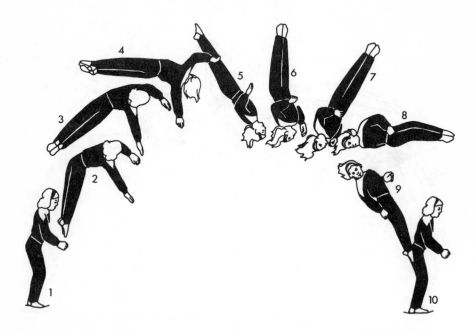

Figure 25—Full Twisting Front Somersault

Evaluation Questions

How would you spot the front cody? the back cody? the double twisting somersault?

twisting front somersault. If a complete twist left is performed, the stomach will be seen first then the back, or back then stomach, depending upon the side from which the performer is viewed.

When using the barani as a basis for learning the full twisting front somersault, one will quite often watch the trampoline too long during the first half of the twist and consequently will land looking over his right shoulder on completion of the twist. The bed should be seen on the start and the finish.

This skill by itself has little value on the trampoline. The value lies in its close association with more advanced twisting skills in which the full twist is either the beginning, the middle, or the ending part of that skill.

Additional Intermediate Skills
1. Three-quarter back somersault, with one-half twist
2. Three-quarter back somersault, with one twist
3. Barani ball out (from back landing, barani to the feet)
4. Full twisting ball out
5. Back over, with one-half twist to back
6. Back over, with one twist to feet
7. One and one-quarter front somersault, one-half twist to back
8. One and three-quarter front somersault to back
9. Back one and one-quarter somersault with one twist to back
10. Three-quarter back somersault with one twist, cody
11. Combinations of intermediate skills
12. Game of add-one

ADVANCED INTERMEDIATE SKILLS

Front Somersault, One and One-Half Twists (twist right to left)

When the somersault begins, the arms reach up as the hips are lifted, pressing the feet up as the body bends forward at the hips. As the bend is made at the hips, the right arm and shoulder is pushed back to the left with the arm bending at the elbow and the hand in close to the body. The performer's head is forcefully rotated to the left and he looks over the left shoulder with his chin tucked but not down as the right arm swings left across the chest. Both arms should start their swing in a wider arc than when performing the full twisting front somersault.

When the hands are pulled in to the body, then their movement is in the opposite direction of the twist, causing a slowing down of the twisting action. Instead of pulling the hands in to one's body, the performer allows the body to turn in to the hands so that they are somewhere in the area of the chest. This action tends to help increase the speed of the twist. In addition, this "body to hands" action or wrap-up is important when learning the more advanced twisting skills.

As the twists increase, the bend at the hips lessens to an almost layout position. Upon completion of the twists, one must flex at the hips

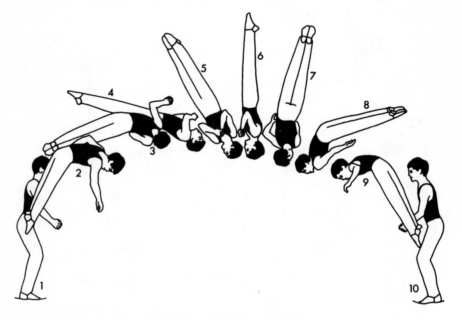

Figure 26—Front Somersault, One and One-Half Twists

with the arms extended to a position fore sideways and lower than shoulder level in preparation for the landing. Prior to landing, the eyes should sight the bed. Do not watch the bed too long on takeoff as this makes it difficult to finish the twisting action in time for a proper landing.

Double Twisting Back Somersault (twist right to left)

The double twisting back somersault may be learned simply by progressing from a full twisting back somersault, then one and one-quarter twists, one and one-half twists, one and three-quarter, and then two twists. This method (the part method) does not require the use of a twisting belt and is quite safe. There are some, however, who can learn twisting kills more easily with a twisting belt than by progression. This "whole method" is used quite successfully by many performers.

The double twisting somersault requires a wrap-up action similar to that of the multiple twisting front somersault. Using the arm action as described for the back somersault with one twist but starting with a wider and more forceful swing of the arms, the same "body to hands" wrap-up technique must be employed as in the performance of the forward somer-

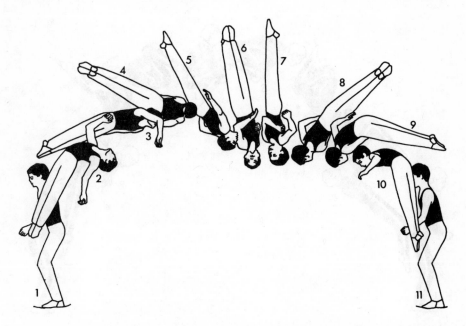

Figure 27—Double Twisting Back Somersault

sault with one and one-half twists. The eyes spot the bed on the start and finish of the twisting action with the point of completion marked with a flexion of the hips. The body position during the performance is a layout.

Caution must be taken with reference to the feet while learning this skill. The tendency is to relax one's ankles and feet, a habit which leads to sprained ankles, twisted knees, and broken bones because of the tremendous torque to which the feet and legs are subjected on landing. The performer should be prepared for the landing with ankles and knees in a state of readiness in order to prevent injury. Another major problem encountered while learning is that of cordinating the twisting action with the somersaulting action. When increasing the speed of the twist, the speed of the somersault is increased, and vice versa. Repetition until the proper timing evolves is the only way of developing the skill properly. The performer must learn to slow down or speed up the twist or somersault without changing the other.

Double Backward Somersault (tuck)

The whole method is used in learning this skill and the overhead safety belt should be put to use.

Figure 28—Double Backward Somersault Tuck

The arms, about shoulder width apart, swing up bent at the elbows. The toes, ankles, and legs extend with force to push the performer upward. As he leaves the bed, he lifts his knees to a flexed position. The legs are lifted, flexed at the knees and at the hips, in the direction of the rotation. The hands catch the legs just below the knees to complete the tuck position. The head is back when the legs are grasped, and the performer must squeeze into a tight tuck. When the one and three-quarter somersault position is reached, the legs are released and extended in preparation for the landing. At this point, the trampoline should come into view. It will be quite some time before the perofrmer becomes aware of where he is. To find the trampoline bed visually will also take time. Since this is the case, the safety belt must be used until both the performer and instructor feel that it is time to remove the belt.

Additional Advanced Intermediate Skills
1. Front double somersault
2. Fliffes (double somersaults with one-half twist)
3. Twisting codys, both front and back
4. Combinations of advanced intermediate skills
5. Doing the same skill in swingtime
6. Game of add-one

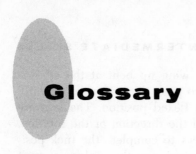

Glossary

ADD-ONE—A game played on the trampoline where each person must do what the preceding person did and then add on a skill.

ALTERNATE BOUNCE—Substitute skill in a prearranged routine.

BABY FLIFFIS—Forward 1¾ somersault to the back, barani to the feet.

BACK—Slang for back somersault.

BACK SOMERSAULT—One complete body revolution around the lateral axis backward.

BACK OVER (Back pull over)—Three-quarter somersault from back takeoff to feet.

BACK TAKEOFF—Starting a skill from back lying position.

BACK TO BACK—Skill starts and ends on the back, also performance of the same skills in swingtime.

BALL OUT—Front somersault action from back drop position.

BARANI (Baranni, baroni, brandy, brani)—One-half twisting front somersault, feet to feet, without losing sight of the bed.

BARANI BALL OUT—Barani action from back takeoff to feet.

BED—A fibrous woven suspended area, usually rectangular, on which skills are performed.

BLIND—A skill which does not allow sighting of the trampoline until just before landing.

BODY TO HANDS—Twisting action where the body twists to the hands rather than pulling the hands in to the body.

BOTTOM—When the bed comes to a sudden stop.

CAST—To lose one's alignment with the trampoline.

CAT TWIST—Back drop, full twist, back drop.

CHECK—Slowing or halting a skill.

CHECK POINT—A sight position on or near the trampoline, which a performer uses to determine his body position while performing a skill or routine.

CHASE—To denote fast rotation of front somersaults.

CLOSE—End of routine.

CODY (cote; codys, plural)—Back or front somersaulting action from the stomach.

CRADLE—One-half twisting, ½ forward somersault from back to back.

CRASH DIVE—Layout front dive position with a last second bend at the hips in order to accomplish a back landing.

DEGREE OF DIFFICULTY—Rating of a skill.

DELTA WING—Type of trampoline bed manufactured by Nissen Corporation.

DISMOUNT—Last skill in a routine; also manner in which one gets off the trampoline.

DOUBLE BACK SOMERSAULT—Two complete body revolutions around the lateral axis backward.

DOUBLE BALL OUT—Double front somersault action from back landing position.

DOUBLE BOUNCE—When one performer assists another by helping to depress the bed.

DOUBLE FRONT SOMERSAULT—Two complete body revolutions around the lateral axis forward.

DOUBLE FULL—Double twisting back somersault.

DOUBLE FULL FRONT—Double twisting front somersault.

DOUBLE SIDE SOMERSAULT—Two complete body revolutions around the dorso-ventral axis.

DOUBLE SOMERSAULT—Two complete body revolutions around the lateral axis front or back.

DOUBLE TURN TABLE—Two consecutive body revolutions around the dorosventral axis while in a prone position.

DOUBLE TWISTING SOMERSAULT—Two complete body revolutions around the longitudinal axis, either right or left with somersault action front or back.

EARLY FLIFFIS—Double somersault with ½ twist in first somersault either front or back.

FLIFFIS (fliffes, plural)—Double somersault with ½ twist front or back.

FLYING SOMERSAULT—Somersault action starting in a layout, then changing to tuck or pike, front or back.

FRAME—Metal frame on which the trampoline bed is suspended.

GLOSSARY

FRAME PAD—Protective padding on the trampoline frame.

FREE—Denotes that body position can be of one's choice (tuck, pike, layout, or pucked) and/or a combination of several positions.

FRONT DROP—Landing position on the stomach.

FRONT SOMERSAULT—One complete body revolution around the lateral axis forward.

FRONT 1 AND 3—Forward 1¾ somersault.

FULL—Back somersault with one twist.

FULL AND ½—Front somersault with 1½ twists.

FULL FRONT—Full twisting front somersault.

FULL TWISTING SOMERSAULT—One complete body rotation around the longitudinal axis either left or right with somersault action front or back.

FUNDAMENTAL BOUNCE—Starting from the feet, landing on the feet with no somersault action.

GAIN—To travel forward on the trampoline bed during the execution of a skill.

HAND BELT—Safety belt held by hand with pieces of rope.

HAND SPOT—Assistance given by a spotter using his hands to insure safety of the performer.

HANDS AND KNEE DROP—Landing on the hands and knees simultaneously.

KILL—To stop bouncing by flexing the knees and absorbing the rebounding action of the trampoline bed.

KIP—From back drop position, body piked, the legs and body are extended up in an arch and forward, legs are then brought down as the shoulders push the bed. Rotation is forward.

KNEE DROP—Landing position with the knees, shin, and instep flat on the bed with back straight and upright.

LATE FLIFFIS—Double somersault with ½ twist in second somersault, front or back.

LAYOUT—Stretched body position with no forward bend.

LEAN—Position of the body in relation to a line perpendicular to the bed of the trampoline.

LOSE—To travel backward on the trampoline bed during the execution of a skill.

MOUNT—First skill of a routine; also manner in which one gets on a trampoline.

NARROW STRAP—Indicates width of straps, usually one inch or less, which are used in the construction of a web trampoline bed.

OPEN PIKE—Body position with legs straight and bent at hips and arms held fore sideways.

OPENER—First skill of a routine.

Evaluation Questions

Are these terms now in your vocabulary: blind, baby fliffis, swingtime, gain, turn table, rudy?

OVER—When body rotates too far around the lateral axis and landing is past the intended point of completion.

PIKE—Body position bent at the waist with legs straight and hands grasping behind the legs in the area of the knees.

PIKE JUMP—A free bounce with body bent at the hips, legs together, straight and parallel with bed.

PRESS—To use steady force in pushing the legs and feet together.

PUCKED—Body position where body is in intermediate position between tuck and pike.

ROLLING TYPE ACTION—Slow twisting action generally done with the knees bent.

ROUTINE—A prescribed number of skills performed consecutively.

RUDOLPH (rudy)—One and a half twisting front somersault.

SAFETY BELT—A belt designed to support the performer while he learns skills in which there is rotation around the lateral axis.

SAFETY PADS—Padding on the frame of a trampoline.

SEAT DROP—Landing on the bed in a sitting position, legs straight, hands by the side.

SHOCK CORDS—Elastic cords, by which the bed is suspended on the frame of the trampoline, which give the rebounding action that lifts the performer.

SHORT—When body does not rotate far enough around the lateral axis and the landing is less than the intended point of completion.

SIDE SOMERSAULT—One complete body revolution around the dorsoventral axis, left or right.

SOMERSAULT—One complete body revolution around the lateral axis, front or back.

GLOSSARY

SPOT—To perform in one localized area of the bed; to focus the eyes on one particular object or spot; to protect another performer.

SPOTTER—A person who protects or spots the performer.

SPREAD—A technique of separating the legs while somersaulting in order to increase the speed of rotation.

STOMACH DROP—Landing on the stomach (prone position).

STRADDLE JUMP—Free bounce with body bent at the hips, legs straight, spread sidewards and parallel with the bed.

SWING OR SWINGTIME—The action of doing one skill right after the other with no intervening free bounce.

SWIVEL HIPS—Seat drop, ½ turn, seat drop.

THREE-QUARTER BACK—Three-quarter body revolution backward around the lateral axis.

THREE-QUARTER FRONT—Three-quarter body revolution forward around the lateral axis.

TRAMPOLINE—An apparatus consisting of a rectangular fibrous woven mat suspended by springs or shock cords which are attached to a stationary rectangular base.

TRAMPOLINING—The sport of performing skills on a trampoline, sometimes referred to as rebound tumbling.

TRAVEL—To move from one area to another on the bed of the trampoline.

TUCK—Body position with knees bent, hips flexed, and hands grasping legs below the knees.

TUCK JUMP—Free jump with knees bent, hips flexed, and hands grasping legs below the knees.

TURN TABLE—One complete body revolution around the dorsoventral axis in a prone position, left or right.

TWIST—One complete body rotation around the longitudinal axis, left or right.

TWISTING BELT—A belt designed to support the performer while learning skills which rotate around each of the three axes or a combination of more than one axis.

WEB BED—Fibrous woven straps usually made of nylon which are suspended by springs or shock cords from the frame of the trampoline.

WEBBING—Straps used in the construction of a trampoline bed.

WHIP BACK—Fast low back somersault in a layout position.

WIDE STRAP—Indicates width of straps, usually 1¾ inches, which are used in the construction of a web trampoline bed.

WRAP-UP—Fast twisting action associated with arms moving in the direction of the twist as in the body to hands technique.

Bibliography

BALEY, JAMES A. *Gymnastics in the School.* Boston, Mass.: Allyn and Bacon, Inc., 1965.

COLE, E. W., H. BILLINGSLEY and R. KAMBALL. *Diving and Rebound Tumbling.* Cedar Rapids, Iowa: Barns Publishing Co., Inc., 1960.

GRISWOLD, LARRY. *Trampoline Tumbling* (second edition). St. Louis: Business Collaborators, Inc., 1948.

HENNESSY, JEFF T. "Rebound Diving," *Aquatics Guide,* DGWS, 1201 Sixteenth St. N.W., Washington 36, D. C.: AAHPER, July 1963-65.

HENNESSY, JEFF T. "The Trampoline and Springboard Diving," *The International Swimmer,* September 1965, Vol. 2, No. 4.

HENNESSY, JEFF T. *The Trampoline . . . As I See It.* Huntsville, Texas: Wide World Publications, 1967.

KEENEY, CHUCK. *Trampolining Illustrated.* New York: The Ronald Press Company, 1961.

LADUE, FRANK and J. NORMAN. *This Is Trampolining* (second edition). Cedar Rapids, Iowa: The Torch Press, 1956.

———. *Two Seconds of Freedom* (fifth edition). Cedar Rapids, Iowa: The Torch Press, 1960.

LOKEN, N. C. and R. J. WILLOUGHBY. *Complete Book of Gymnastics.* Englewood Cliffs, New Jersey: Prentice-Hall, Inc., 1959. Second edition, 1967.

LUCCHESI, CHUCK. "Diving the Trampoline Way!," *Scholastic Coach,* December, 1952.

RUFF, WESLEY K. *Gymnastics Beginner to Competitor.* Dubuque, Iowa: Wm. C. Brown Co. Publishers, 1959.

BIBLIOGRAPHY

SEATON, D., I. CLAYTON, H. LEIBEE and L. MESSERSMITH. *Physical Education Handbook* (fourth edition). Englewood Cliffs, New Jersey: Prentice-Hall, Inc., 1965.

STANLEY, D. K. and I. F. WAGLOW. *Physical Education Activities Handbook for Men and Women* (second edition). Boston, Mass.: Allyn & Bacon, Inc., 1966.

U. S. NAVAL INSTITUTE, *Gymnastics and Tumbling* (second edition). New York: The Ronald Press Company, 1959.

TRAMPOLINE RULE BOOKS

International Trampoline Federation
6 Frankfurt M.-Niederrad
Otto Fleck-Schneise, West Germany

NAAU Gymnastic Guide
231 West 58th Street
New York, New York 10019

NCAA Official Gymnastic Rules
Box 757 Grand Central Station
New York, New York 10000

NAIA Gymnastic Rules
106 West 12th Street
Kansas City, Missouri 64105

AUDIO-VISUAL AIDS FOR TRAMPOLINING

The Athletic Institute
805 Merchandise Mart
Chicago, Illinois 60654

American Athletic Equipment Co.
Jefferson, Iowa 50129
"Basic Trampoline Skills"

Jeff T. Hennessy, Box 672, University of Southwestern Louisiana
Lafayette, Louisiana 70501
"U. S. Trampoline Champions in Action" (2nd edition), 1966
"Third World Trampoline Championships," 1966

Nissen Corporation
930 27th Ave., S.W.
Cedar Rapids, Iowa 52406
"Up In the Air," "Introducing the Trampoline"
"1967 World Professional Trampoline Championships"

TEACHING AIDS FOR TRAMPOLINING (wall charts)

American Athletic Equipment Co.
Jefferson, Iowa 50129

Gym Master
3200 South Zuni Street
Englewood, Colorado 80110

Nissen Corporation
930 27th Ave., S.W.
Cedar Rapids, Iowa 52406

Porter Athletic Equipment
9555 Iriving Park Road
Schiller Park, Illinois 60176

Appendix

RECOMMENDATIONS FOR PURCHASING A TRAMPOLINE

When purchasing a trampoline, the following should be considered:

1. The larger type trampoline is by far the best for both instruction and competition. The additional surface area on which to work provides a wider margin for safety and affords a better teaching and learning environment. The student is more at ease on the larger bed and therefore tends to learn more rapidly.

2. The 1″ nylon web bed produces a rebound action necessary for learning. The 1¾″ nylon web and the solid bed do not produce enough rebound and are not adequate for teaching, learning or competition.

3. Springs are cheaper and last longer than rubber cables. In addition, they give a more uniform action which is necessary for good control.

4. All trampolines should be equipped with frame pads for safety purposes.

5. Roller stands should be standard equipment so that the trampoline can be folded and transported with ease.

6. Folding-type trampolines should be purchased to insure the long life of the suspension system and to provide ease in storing.

7. Maintenance recommendations of the manufacturer should be strictly observed.

Index